Letters Of John Quincy Adams, To His Son, On The Bible And Its Teachings

LETTERS

OF

JOHN QUINCY ADAMS,

TO HIS SON,

ON

THE BIBLE AND ITS TEACHINGS.

Auburn, N. Y.:

DERBY, MILLER, & CO.

1849.

Entered, according to Act of Congress, in 1848,

By DERBY, MILLER, & CO.,

in the Clerk's Office of the District Court of the
U. S., for the Northern District of New York.

Stereotyped by Redfield & Savage,
13 Chambers Street, N. Y.

TO THE

YOUNG MEN

OF

AMERICA

THIS LITTLE VOLUME

Is Respectfully

INSCRIBED.

PREFACE.

JOHN QUINCY ADAMS, the writer of the following Letters, is widely known as one of the purest and most eminent men of our age. Born in 1767, during the fierce and absorbing discussions of the rights and responsibilities of rulers which heralded our Revolution and war of Independence, he entered his country's service, while yet a mere lad, as secretary to the Russian embassy, and remained through life, with few and brief intermissions, a public servant, filling successively the posts of secretary, embassador, United States senator, negotiator of the last treaty of peace with Great Britain, secretary of state, president, and finally representative in Congress, which station he filled from 1831 to the hour of his death, which took place in the Capitol, February 23, 1848, he having been stricken down with paralysis, while in the act of rising to address the house, two days before; having lived more than eighty years, and passed nearly or quite three fourths of his days in public stations. Though naturally reserved and diffident in manner, and never in the obvious sense a popular man — for his life was devoted to serving rather than pleasing his countrymen — he was profoundly and generally esteemed for his fearless conscientiousness, his ardent patriotism, his vast and various acquirements, and his unfaltering devotion to human freedom. The funeral honors paid to his memory have had no parallel in this country, except in the case of Washington. Those who had seen fit to oppose his election and to defeat his re-election as president, and to whom he had generally stood opposed in party differences, seemed to vie with his warmest supporters in rendering homage to his memory.

The following letters were written by Mr. Adams, while embassador at St. Petersburgh, to one of his sons, who was at school in Massachusetts. Their purpose is the inculcation of a love and reverence for the Holy Scriptures, and a delight in their perusal and study. Throughout his long life, Mr. Adams was himself a daily and devout reader of the Scriptures, and delighted in comparing and considering them in the various languages with which he was familiar, hoping thereby to acquire a nicer and clearer appreciation of their meaning. The Bible was emphatically his counsel and monitor through life, and the fruits of its guidance are seen in the unsullied character which he bore through the turbid waters of political contention to his final earthly rest. Though long and fiercely opposed and contemned in life, he left no man behind him who would wish to fix a stain on the name he has inscribed so high on the roll of his country's most gifted and illustrious sons.

The intrinsic value of these letters, their familiar and lucid style, their profound and comprehensive views, their candid and reverent spirit, must win for them a large measure of the public attention and esteem. But, apart from even this, the testimony so unconsciously borne by their pure-minded and profoundly learned author to the truth and excellence of the Christian faith and records, will not be lightly regarded. It is no slight testimonial to the verity and worth of Christianity, that in all ages since its promulgation, the great mass of those who have risen to eminence by their profound wisdom, integrity, and philanthropy, have recognised and reverenced in Jesus of Nazareth, the Son of the living God. To the names of Augustine, Xavier, Fenelon, Milton, Newton, Locke, Lavater, Howard, Chateaubriand, and their thousands of compeers in Christian faith, among the world's wisest and noblest, it is not without pride that the American may add, from among his countrymen, those of such men as WASHINGTON, JAY, PATRICK HENRY, and JOHN QUINCY ADAMS.

THE BIBLE AND ITS TEACHINGS.

~~~~~~~~~~~~~~~~~~~~~~~~

LETTER I.

St. Petersburg, *Sept.*, 1811.

MY DEAR SON: In your letter of the 18th January to your mother, you mentioned that you read to your aunt a chapter in the Bible or a section of Doddridge's Annotations every evening. This information gave me real pleasure; for so great is my veneration for the Bible, and so strong my belief, that when duly read and meditated on, it is of all books in the world, that which contributes most to make men good, wise, and happy—that the earlier my children begin to read it, the more steadily they pursue the practice of reading it throughout their lives, the more lively and confident will be my hopes that they will prove useful citizens to their country, respectable members of society, and a real blessing to their parents. But I hope you have now arrived at an age to understand that reading, even in the Bible, is a thing in itself, neither good nor bad, but that all the good which can be drawn from it, is by the use and improvement of what you have read, with the help of your own reflection. Young people sometimes boast of how many books, and how much they have read; when, instead of boasting, they ought to be ashamed of having wasted so much time, to so little profit.

I advise you, my son, in whatever you read, and most of all in reading the Bible, to remember that it is for the purpose of making you wiser and more virtuous. I have myself, for many years,

made it a practice to read through the
Bible once every year. I have always
endeavored to read it with the same spirit
and temper of mind, which I now recommend to you : that is, with the intention
and desire that it may contribute to my
advancement in wisdom and virtue. My
desire is indeed very imperfectly success-
ful; for, like you, and like the Apostle
Paul, " I find a law in my members, war-
ring against the laws of my mind." But
as I know that it is my nature to be imperfect, so I know that it is my duty to aim at
perfection; and feeling and deploring my
own frailties, I can only pray Almighty
God, for the aid of his Spirit to strength-
en my good desires, and to subdue my
propensities to evil; for it is from him,
that every good and every perfect gift
descends. My custom is, to read four or
five chapters every morning, immediately
after rising from my bed. It employs

about an hour of my time, and seems to me the most suitable manner of beginning the day. But, as other cares, duties, and occupations, engage the remainder of it, I have perhaps never a sufficient portion of my time in meditation, upon what I have read. Even meditation itself is often fruitless, unless it has some special object in view; useful thoughts often arise in the mind, and pass away without being remembered or applied to any good purpose—like the seed scattered upon the surface of the ground, which the birds devour, or the wind blows away, or which rot without taking root, however good the soil may be upon which they are cast. We are all, my dear George, unwilling to confess our own faults, even to ourselves : and when our own consciences are too honest to conceal them from us, our self-love is always busy,. either in attempting to disguise them to us under false and delusive colors, or in seeking out excuses and apologies to reconcile them to our minds. Thus, although I am sensible that I have not derived from my assiduous perusal of the Bible (and I might apply the same remark to almost everything else that I do) all the benefit that I might and ought, I am as constantly endeavoring to persuade myself that it is not my own fault. Sometimes I say to myself, I do not understand what I have read; I can not help it; I did not make my own understanding: there are many things in the Bible "hard to understand," as St. Peter expressly says of Paul's epistles: some are hard in the Hebrew, and some in the Greek—the original languages in which the Scriptures were written; some are harder still in the translations. I have been obliged to lead a wandering life about the world, and scarcely ever have at hand the book, which might help me to surmount these difficulties. Conscience sometimes puts the question—whether my not understanding many passages is not owing to my want of attention in reading them. I must admit, that it is; a full proof of which is, that every time I read the Book through, I understand some passages which I never understood before, and which I should have done, at a former reading, had it been effected with a sufficient degree of attention. Then, in answer to myself, I say: It is true; but I can not always command my own attention, and never can to the degree that I wish. My mind is ofttimes so full of other things, absorbed in bodily pain, or engrossed by passion, or distracted by pleasure, or exhausted by dissipation, that I can not give to proper daily employment the attention which I gladly would, and which is absolutely necessary

to make it "fruitful of good works."
This acknowledgment of my weakness
is just; but for how much of it I am still
accountable to God, I hardly dare acknowledge to myself. Is it bodily pain?
How often was that brought upon me by
my own imprudence or folly? Was it
passion? Heaven has given to every
human being, the power of controlling
his passions, and if-he neglects or loses
it, the fault is his own, and he must be
answerable for it. Was it pleasure?
Why did I indulge it? Was it dissipation? This is the most inexcusable of
all; for it must have been occasioned by
my own thoughtlessness or irresolution.
It is of no use to discover our own
faults and infirmities, unless the discovery
prompts us to amendment.

I have thought if in addition to the
hour which I daily give to the reading of
the Bible, I should also from time to time

(and especially on the Sabbath) apply another hour occasionally to communicate to you the reflections that arise in my mind upon its perusal, it might not only tend to fix and promote my own attention to the excellent instructions of that sacred Book, but perhaps also assist your advancement in its knowledge and wisdom. At your age, it is probable that you have still greater difficulties to understand all that you read in the Bible, than I have at mine; and if you have so much self-observation as your letters indicate, you will be sensible of as much want of attention, both voluntary and involuntary, as I here acknowledge in myself. I intend, therefore, for the purpose of contributing to your improvement and my own, to write you several letters, in due time to follow this, in which I shall endeavor to show you how you may derive the most advantage to yourself, from the perusal of the Scriptures. It is probable, when you receive these letters, you will not, at first reading entirely understand them ; if that should be the case, ask your grand-parents, or your uncle or aunt, to explain them : if you still find them too hard, put them on file, and lay them by for two or three years, after which read them again, and you will find them easy enough. It is essential, my son, in order that you may go through life with comfort to yourself, and usefulness to your fellow-creatures, that you should form and adopt certain rules or principles, for the government of your own conduct and temper. Unless you have such rules and principles, there will be numberless occasions on which you will have no guide for your government but your passions. In your infancy and youth, you have been, and will be for some years, under the authority and con-

trol of your friends and instructors ; but
you must soon come to the age when you
must govern yourself. You have already
come to that age in many respects ; you
know the difference between right and
wrong, and you know some of your duties, and the obligations you are under,
to become acquainted with them all. It
is in the Bible, you must learn them, and
from the Bible how to practise them.
Those duties are to God, to your fellow-
creatures, and to yourself. " Thou shalt
love the Lord thy God, with all thy
heart, and with all thy soul, and with all
thy mind, and with all thy strength, and
thy neighbor as thyself."   On these two
commandments, Jesus Christ expressly
says, " hang all the law and the prophets ;" that is to say, the whole purpose
of Divine Revelation is to inculcate them
efficaciously upon the minds of men.
You will perceive that I have spoken of

duties to *yourself*, distinct from those to God and to your fellow-creatures; while Jesus Christ speaks only of two commandments. The reason is, because Christ, and the commandments repeated by him, consider self-love as so implanted in the heart of every man by the law of his nature, that it requires no commandment to establish its influence over the heart; and so great do they know its power to be, that they demand no other measure for the love of our neighbor, than that which they know we shall have for ourselves. But from the love of God, and the love of our neighbor, result duties to ourselves as well as to them, and they are all to be learned in equal perfection by our searching the Scriptures.

Let us, then, search the Scriptures; and, in order to pursue our inquiries with methodical order, let us consider the various sources of information, that we may draw from in this study. The Bible contains the revelation of the will of God. It contains the history of the creation of the world, and of mankind; and afterward the history of one peculiar nation, certainly the most extraordinary nation that has ever appeared upon the earth. It contains a system of religion, and of morality, which we may examine upon its own merits, independent of the sanction it receives from being the Word of God; and it contains a numerous collection of books, written at different ages of the world, by different authors, which we may survey as curious monuments of antiquity, and as literary compositions. In what light soever we regard it, whether with reference to revelation, to literature, to history, or to morality — it is an invaluable and inexhaustible mine of knowledge and virtue.

I shall number separately those letters that I mean to write you upon the subject of the Bible, and as, after they are finished, I shall perhaps ask you to read them all together, or to look over them again myself, you must keep them on separate file. I wish that hereafter they may be useful to your brothers and sisters, as well as to you. As you will receive them as a token of affection for you, during my absence, I pray that they may be worthy to read by them all with benefit to themselves, if it please God, that they should live to be able to understand them.

From your affectionate Father,
JOHN QUINCY ADAMS.

LETTER II.

THE first point of view in which I have invited you to consider the Bible, is in the light of *Divine Revelation.* And what are we to understand by these terms? I intend as much as possible, to avoid the field of controversy, which I am not well acquainted with, and for which I have little respect, and still less inclination. My idea of the Bible as a *Divine Revelation,* is founded upon its practical use to mankind, and not upon metaphysical subtleties. There are three points of doctrine, the belief of which, forms the foundation of all morality. The first is, the existence of a God; the second is the immortality of the human soul; and the third is, a future state of rewards and punishments. Suppose it possible for a man to disbelieve either of these articles of faith, and that man will have no conscience, he will have no other law than that of the tiger or the shark; the laws of man may bind him in chains, or may put him to death, but they never can make him wise, virtuous, or happy. It is possible to believe them all without believing that the Bible is a Divine revelation. It is so obvious to every reasonable being, that he did not make himself, and the world which he inhabits, could as little make itself, that the moment we begin to exercise the power of reflection, it seems impossible to escape the conviction that there is a Creator. It is equally evident that the Creator must be a spiritual, and not a material being; there is also a consciousness that the thinking part of our nature is not material, but spiritual—that it is not subject to the laws of matter, nor perishable with it. Hence arises the belief, that we have an immortal soul; and pursuing the train of thought which the visible creation and observation upon ourselves suggest, we must soon discover that the Creator must also be the Governor of the universe; that his wisdom, and his goodness, must be without bounds—that he is a righteous God, and loves righteousness—that mankind are bound by the laws of righteousness, and are accountable to him for their obedience to them in this life, according to their good or evil deeds. This completion of Divine justice must be reserved for another life. The existence of a Creator, the immortality of the human soul, and a future state of retribution, are therefore so perfectly congenial to natural reason when once discov-

ered—or rather it is so impossible for
natural reason to disbelieve them—that
it would seem the light of natural reason
could alone suffice for their discovery;
but the conclusion would not be correct.
Human reason may be sufficient to get
an obscure glimpse of these sacred and
important truths, but it can not discover
them, in all their clearness. For example;—in all their numberless, false reli-
gions, which have swayed the minds of
men in different ages, and regions of the
world, the idea of a God has always
been included:—

> "Father of all! in every age,
> In every clime adored—
> By saint, by savage, and by sage—
> Jehovah, Jove, or Lord."

So says Pope's Universal Prayer.' But,
it is the God of the Hebrews alone, who
is announced to us as the Creator of the
world. The ideas of God entertained by

all the most illustrious and most ingenious nations of antiquity were weak and
absurd. The Persians worshipped the
sun; the Egyptians believed in an innu-
merable multitude of gods, and worshipped not only oxen, crocodiles, dogs, and
cats, but even garlics and onions. The
Greeks invented a poetical religion, and
adored men and women, virtues and
vices, air, water, and fire, and everything
that a vivid imagination could personify.
Almost all the Greek philosophers reason-
ed and meditated upon the nature of the
gods; but scarcely any of them reflected
enough even to imagine that there was
but one God, and not one of them ever
conceived of him as the Creator of the
world. Cicero has collected together all
their opinions upon the nature of the gods,
and pronounced them more like the dreams
of madmen than the sober judgment of
wise men. In the first book of Ovid's

Metamorphoses, there is an account of the change of chaos in the world. Before the sea, and the earth, and the sky that surrounds all things (says Ovid), there was a thing called chaos, and some of the gods (he does not know which), separated from each other the elements of this chaos, and turned them into the world; thus far and no farther could human reason extend. But the first words of the Bible are, "In the beginning God created the heavens and the earth." The blessed and sublime idea of God, as the creator of the universe, the source of all human happiness for which all the sages and philosophers of Greece and Rome groped in darkness and never found, is recalled in the first verse of the book of Genesis. I call it the source of all human virtue and happiness; because when we have attained the conception of a Being, who by the mere act of his will, created the world, it would follow as an irresistible consequence—even if we were not told that the same Being must also be the governor of his own creation—that man, with all other things, was also created by him, and must hold his felicity and virtue on the condition of obedience to his will. In the first chapters of the Bible there is a short and rapid historical narrative of the manner in which the world and man were made—of the condition upon which happiness and immortality were bestowed upon our first parents—of their transgression of this condition—of the punishment denounced upon them—and the promise of redemption from it by the " seed of the woman."

There are, and always have been, where the Holy Scriptures have been known, petty witlings and self-conceited reasoners, who cavil at some of the particular details of this narration. Even serious inquirers after truth have sometimes been perplexed to believe that there should have been evening and morning before the existence of the sun—that man should be made of clay, and woman from the ribs of man—that they should have been forbidden to eat an apple, and for disobedience to that injunction, be with all their posterity doomed to death, and that eating an apple could give "the knowledge of good and evil"—that a serpent should speak and beguile a woman. All this is undoubtedly marvellous, and above our comprehension. Much of it is clearly figurative and allegorical; nor is it easy to distinguish what part of it is to be understood in a literal and not in a symbolical sense. But all that it imports us to know or understand is plain; the great and essential principles, upon which our duties and enjoyments depend, are involved in no obscurity. A God, the

Creator and Governor of the universe, is revealed in all his majesty and power; the terms upon which he gave existence and happiness to the common parent of mankind are exposed to us in the clearest light. Disobedience to the will of God was the offence for which he was precipitated from paradise : obedience to the will of God is the merit by which paradise is to be regained. Here, then, is the foundation of all morality—the source of all our obligations, as accountable creatures. This idea of the transcendent power of the Supreme Being is essentially connected with that by which the whole duty of man is summed up; obedience to his will. I have observed that natural reason might suffice for an obscure perception, but not for the clear discovery of these truths. Even Cicero could start to his own mind the question, whether justice could exist upon earth

unless founded upon piety, but could not
settle it to his own satisfaction. The ray
of divine light contained in the principle,
that justice has no other foundation than
piety, could make its way to the soul of
the heathen, but there it was extinguish-
ed in the low, unsettled, and inconsistent
notions which were the only foundations
of *his* piety. How could his piety be
pure or sound, when he did not know
whether there was one God or a thousand
—whether he, or they had or had not any
concern in the formation of the world, and
whether they had any regard to the affairs or the conduct of mankind? Once
assume the idea of a single God, the Creator of all things, whose will is the law
of moral obligation to man, and to whom
man is accountable, and piety becomes
as rational as it is essential; it becomes
the first of human duties; and not a doubt
can henceforth remain, that fidelity in the

associations of human piety, and that most excellent virtue, justice, repose upon no other foundation.

At a later age than Cicero, Longinus expressly quotes the third verse of the first chapter of Genesis as an example of the sublime. "And God said let there be light, and there was light;" and wherein consists its sublimity? In the image of the transcendent power presented to the mind, with the most striking simplicity of expression. Yet this verse only exhibits the effects of that transcendent power which the first verse discloses in announcing God as the Creator of the world. The true sublimity is in the idea given us of God. To such a God the heart of man must yield with cheerfulness the tribute of homage which it never could pay to the numerous gods of Egypt, to the dissolute debauchees of the heathen mythology, nor even to the more elevated, but not less fantastical imaginations of the Grecian philosophers and sages.

From your affectionate Father,
JOHN QUINCY ADAMS.

LETTER III.

THE second general point of view, in which I propose for you to consider the Bible, to the end that it may " thoroughly furnish you unto all good works," is in the historical character. ·

To a man of liberal education, the study of history is not only useful, and important, but altogether indispensable, and with regard to the history contained in the Bible, the observation which Cicero makes respecting that of his own country is much more emphatically applicable, that "it is not so much praiseworthy to be acquainted with as it is shameful to be ignorant of it." History, so far as it relates to the actions and adventures of men, may be divided into five different classes. First, the history of the world, otherwise called universal history; second, that of particular nations; third, that of particular institutions; fourth, that of single families; and fifth, that of individual men. The last two of these classes are generally distinguished by the name of memoirs and biography. All these classes of history are to be found in the Bible, and it may be worth your while to discriminate them one from another. The universal history is short, and all contained in the first eleven chapters of Genesis, together with the first chapter of the first book of Chronicles, which is little more than a genealogical list of names; but it is of great importance, not only as it includes the history of the creation, of the fall of man, of the antediluvian world, and the flood by which the whole human race (excepting Noah and his family) were destroyed, but as it gives a very precise account of the time from the creation until the birth of Abraham. This is the foundation of ancient history, and in reading profane historians hereafter, I would advise you always to reflect upon their narratives with reference to it with respect to the chronology. A correct idea of this is so necessary to understand all history, ancient and modern, that 1 may hereafter write you something further concerning it: for the present I shall only recommend to your particular attention the fifth and eleventh chapters of Genesis, and request you to cast up and write me the amount of the age of the world when Abraham was born. The remainder of the book of Genesis, beginning at the twelfth chapter, is a history of one individual (Abraham) and his family during three generations of his descendants,

after which the book of Exodus com-
mences with the history of the same family, multiplied into a nation; this national and family history is continued through
the books of the Old Testament until that
of Job, which is of a peculiar character,
differing in many particulars from every
other part of the Scriptures. There is
no other history extant which can give
so interesting and correct view of the rise
and progress of human associations, as
this account of Abraham and his descendants, through all the vicissitudes to which
individuals, families, and nations, are lia-
ble. There is no other history where
the origin of a whole nation is traced up
to a single man, and where a connected
train of events and a regular series of
persons from generation to generation is
preserved. As the history of a family,
it is intimately connected with our religious principles and opinions, for it is

the family from which (in his human
character) Jesus Christ descended. It
begins by relating the commands of God
to Abraham, to abandon his country, his
kindred, and his father's house; and to
go to a land which he would show him.
This command was accompanied by two
promises; from which, and from their
fulfilment, arose the differences which I
have just noticed between the history of
the Jews and that of every other nation.
The first of these promises was that
" God would make Abraham a great nation, and bless him ;" the second, and incomparably the most important was, that
"in him all the families of the earth should
be blessed." This promise was made
about two thousand years before the birth
of Christ, and in him had its fulfilment.
When Abraham, in obedience to the command of God, had gone into the land of
Canaan, the Lord appeared unto him and

made him a third promise, which was
that he should give that land to a nation
which should descend from him, as a
possession: this was fulfilled between
five and six hundred years afterward.
In reading all the historical books of
both the Old and the New Testament, as
well as the books of the prophets, you
should always bear in mind the reference
which they have to these three promises
of God to Abraham. All the history is
no more than a narrative of the particular manner, and the detail of events by
which those promises were fulfilled.

In the account of the creation, and the
fall of man, I have already remarked that
the moral doctrine inculcated by the Bible is, that the great consummation of all
human virtue consists in obedience to the
will of God. When we come hereafter
to speak of the Bible in its ethical character, I shall endeavor to show you the

intrinsic excellence of this principle; but
I shall now only remark how strongly
the principle itself is illustrated, first in
the account of the fall, and next by the
history of Abraham.   In the account of
the creation we are informed that God,
after having made the world, created the
first human pair, and " gave them dominion over every living thing that moveth
upon the earth."   He gave them also
" every herb bearing seed, and the fruit
of every tree for meat;" and all this we
are told " God saw was very good."
Thus the immediate possession of everything was given them, and its perpetual
enjoyment secured to their descendants,
on condition of abstaining from the " fruit
of the tree of knowledge of good and
evil."   It is altogether immaterial to my
present remarks whether the narrative is
to be understood in a literal or allegorical
sense, as not only the *knowledge*, but the

possession of created good was granted;
the fruit of the tree, could confer upon
them no knowledge but that of evil, and
the command was nothing more than to
abstain from that knowledge—to forbear
from rushing upon their own destruction.
It is not sufficient to say that this was a
command in its own nature light and easy;
it wás a command to pursue the only law
of their nature, to keep the happiness that
had been heaped upon them without measure; but observe—it contained the principle of *obedience*—it was assigned to
them as a duty—and the heaviest of
penalties was denounced upon its transgression. They were not to discuss the
wisdom, or justice of this command; they
were not to inquire why it had been enjoined upon them, nor could they have
the slightest possible motive for the in-
quiry: unqualified . felicity and immortality were already theirs; wretchedness

and death were alone forbidden them, but placed within their reach as merely trials of their obedience. They violated the law; they forfeited their joy and immortality; they "brought into the world, death, and all our wo." Here, then, is an extreme case in which the mere principle of obedience could be tried, and command to abstain from that from which every motive of reason and interest would have deterred had the command never been given—a command given in the easiest of all possible form, requiring not so much as an action of any kind, but merely forbearance; and its transgression was so severely punished, the only inference we can draw from it is that the most aggravated of all crimes, and that which includes in itself all others, is disobedience to the will of God.

Let us now consider how the principle of obedience is inculcated in the history of Abraham, by a case in the opposite extreme. God commanded Abraham to abandon for ever his country, his kindred, and his father's house, to go, he knew not where; promising, as a reward of his obedience, to bless him and his posterity, though he was then childless: he was required to renounce everything that could most contribute to the happiness and comfort of his life, and which was in his actual enjoyment; to become a houseless, friendless wanderer upon the earth, on the mere faith of the promise that a land should be shown him which his descendants should possess—that they should be a great nation—and that through them all mankind should receive in future ages a blessing. The obedience required of Adam, was merely to retain all the blessings he enjoyed; the obedience of Abraham was to sacrifice all that be possessed for the vague and distant prospect of a

future compensation to his posterity : the
self-control and self-denial required of
Adam, was in itself the slightest that imagination can conceive—but its failure
was punished by the forfeiture of all his
enjoyments ; the self-dominion to be ex-
ercised by Abraham was of the most se-
vere and painful kind—but its accom-
plishment will ultimately be rewarded by
the restoration of all that was forfeited by
Adam.   This restoration, however, was
to be obtained by no ordinary proof of
obedience; the sacrifice of mere personal
blessings, however great, could not lay
the foundation for the redemption of mankind from death ; the voluntary submission of Jesus Christ to his own death, in
the most excruciating and ignominious
form, was to consummate the great plan
of redemption, but the submission of
Abraham to sacrifice his beloved, and only
son Isaac—the child promised by God

himself, and through whom all the greater promises were to be carried into effect,
the feelings of nature, the parent's bowels,
were all required to be sacrified by Abraham to the blind unquestioning principle
of obedience to the will of God. The
blood of Isaac was not indeed shed—the
butchery of an only son by the hand of
his father, was a sacrifice which a merciful God did not require to be complete-
ly executed; but as an instance of obedience it was imposed upon Abraham,
and nothing less than the voice of an
angel from heaven could arrest his up-
lifted arm, and withhold him from sheath-
ing his knife in the heart of his child. It
was upon this testimonial of obedience,
that God's promise of redemption was expressly renewed to Abraham: "In thy
seed shall all the nations of the earth be
blessed, because thou hast obeyed my
voice."—Genesis xxii. 18.

LETTER IV.

WE were considering the Bible in its historical character, and as the history of a family. From the moment when the universal history finishes, that of Abraham begins, and thenceforth, it is the history of a family, of which Abraham is the first, and Jesus Christ the last person; and from the first appearance of Abraham, the whole history appears to have been ordered from age to age, expressly to prepare for the appearance of Christ upon earth. The history begins with the first and mildest trials of Abraham's obedience, and the promise as a reward of his fidelity, that "in him all the

families of the earth should be blessed."
The second trial, which required the sacrifice of his son, was many years afterward, and the promise was more explicit,
and more precisely assigned as the reward of his *obedience*. There were between these periods, two intermediate
occasions, recorded in the fifteenth and
eighteenth chapters of Genesis — on the
first of which, the word of the Lord
came to Abraham in a vision, and promised him he should have a child, from
whom a great and mighty nation should
proceed, which, after being in servitude
four hundred years in a strange land,
should become the possessors of the land
of Canaan, from that of Egypt, to the
river Euphrates. On the second, the
Lord appeared to him and his wife, repeated the promise, that they should
have a child, that "Abraham should
surely become a great nation," and that

"all the nations of the earth should be blessed in him," "for I know him, saith the Lord, that he will command his household after him, and that they will keep the way of the Lord, to do justice and judgment, that the Lord may bring upon Abraham that which he hath spoken of him :" from all which it is obvious that the first of the promises was made as subservient and instrumental to the second — that the great and mighty nation was to be raised as the means in the ways of God's providence, for producing the sacred person of Jesus Christ, through whom the perfect sacrifice of atonement for the original transgression of man should be consummated, and by which "all the families of the earth should be blessed." I am so little versed in controversial divinity, that I know not whether this eighteenth chapter of Genesis, has ever been adduced in support of the doctrine of Trinity ; there is at least in it an alteration of those divine persons, and of one not a little remarkable which I know not how to explain ; if taken in connexion with the nineteenth, it would seem that one of the men entertained by Abraham, was God himself, and the other two were angels, sent to destroy Sodom.

Leaving this, however, let me ask your particular attention, to the reason assigned by God for bestowing such extraordinary blessings upon Abraham. It unfolds to us the first and most important part of the superstructure of moral principle, erected upon the foundation of obedience to the will of God. The rigorous trials of Abraham's obedience mentioned in this, and my last letter, were only tests to ascertain his character in reference to the single, and I may say abstract point of obedience. Here we have a precious gleam of light, disclosing what

the nature of this will of God was, that
he should command his children, and his
household after him; by which the pa-
rental authority to instruct, and direct
his descendants in the way of the Lord
was given him as an authority, and enjoined upon him as a duty; and the lessons which he was then empowered and
required to teach his posterity were, "to
do justice and judgment." Thus, as obedience to the will of God, is the first,
and all-comprehensive virtue taught in
the Bible, so the second is justice and
judgment toward mankind; and this is
exhibited as the result naturally following
from the other. In the same chapter is
related the intercession of Abraham with
God for the preservation of Sodom from
destruction: the city was destroyed for
its crimes, but the Lord promised Abraham it should be spared, if only ten righteous should be found in it: the principle

of mercy was therefore sanctioned in immediate connexion with that of justice. Abraham had several children; but the great promise of God was to be performed through Isaac alone, and of the two sons of Isaac, Jacob—the youngest—was selected for the foundation of the second family and nation; it was from Jacob that the multiplication of the family began, and his twelve sons, were all included in the genealogy of the tribes which afterward constituted the Jewish people. Ishmael, the children of Keturah, and Esau, the eldest son of Isaac, were all the parents of considerable families, which afterward spread into nations; but they formed no part of the chosen people, and their history, with that of the neighboring nations, is only incidentally noticed in the Bible, so far as they had relations of intercourse or hostility with the people of God.

The history of Abraham and his descendants to the close of the book of Genesis is a biography of individuals : the incidents related of them are all of the class belonging to domestic life. Joseph, indeed, became a highly distinguished public character in the land of Egypt, and it was through him that his father and all his brothers were finally settled there — which was necessary to prepare for the existence of their posterity as a nation, and to fulfil the purpose which God had announced to Abraham, that they should be four hundred years dwellers in a strange land. In the lives of Abraham, Isaac, Jacob, and Joseph, many miraculous events are recorded ; but all those which are spoken of as happening in the ordinary course of human affairs have an air of reality about them which no invention could imitate. In some of the transactions related, the conduct of the patriarchs is highly blameable; circumstances of deep depravity are particularly told of Reuben, Simeon, Levi, and Judah, upon which it is necessary to remark that their actions are never spoken of with approbation, but always with strong marks of censure, and generally with a minute account of the punishment which followed upon their transgression. The vices and crimes of the patriarchs, are sometimes alleged as objections against the belief that persons guilty of them should ever have been especially favored by God; but, vicious as they were, there is every reason to be convinced that they were less so than their contemporaries: their vices appear to us at this day gross, disgusting and atrocious; but the written law was not then given, the boundaries between right and wrong were not defined with the same precision as in the tables given afterward to Moses; the law of nature was the only rule of morality by which they could be governed, and the sins of intemperance, of every kind recorded in Holy Writ, were at that period less aggravated than they have been in after ages, because they were in great measure sins of ignorance. From the time when the sons of Jacob were settled in Egypt until the completion of the four hundred years, during which God had foretold to Abraham that his family should dwell there, there is a chasm in the sacred history. We are expressly told that all the house of Jacob which came into Egypt, were threescore and ten: it is said then that Joseph died, as did all that generation; after which nothing further is related of their posterity than that " they were faithful and multiplied abundantly, and waxed exceeding mighty, and the land was filled with them, until there arose a new king who knew not Joseph."—On his first arrival in

Egypt, Jacob had obtained a grant from Pharaoh of the land of Goshen, a place particularly suited to the pasturage of flocks : Jacob and his family were shepherds, and this circumstance was, in the first instance, the occasion upon which that separate spot was assigned to them, and, secondarily, was the means provided by God for keeping separate two nations thus residing together: every shepherd was an abomination to the Egyptians, and the Israelites were shepherds, although dwelling in the land of Egypt; therefore, the Israelites were sojourners and strangers; and by mutual antipathy toward each other, originating in their respective conditions, they were prevented from intermingling by marriage, and losing their distinctive characters. This was the cause which had been reserved by the Supreme Creator, during the space of three generations and more

than four centuries, as the occasion for
eventually bringing them out of the land;
for, in proportion as they multiplied, it
had the tendency to excite the jealousies
and fears of the Egyptian king—as ac-
tually happened. These jealousies and
fears suggested to him a policy of the
most intolerable oppression and the most
execrable cruelty toward the Israelites:
not contented with reducing them to the
most degraded condition of servitude, and
making their lives bitter with hard bond-
age, he conceived the project of destroy-
ing the whole race, by ordering all the
male children to be murdered as soon as
they were born. In the wisdom of Providence, this very command was the means
of preparing this family—when they had
multiplied into a nation—for their issue
from Egypt, and for their conquest of the
land which had been promised to Abraham; and it was at the same time the

immediate occasion of raising up the great warrior, legislator, and prophet, who was to be their deliverer and leader. Thenceforth, they are to be considered as a people, and their history as that of a nation. During a period of more than a thousand years, the Bible gives us a particular account of their destinies : an outline of their constitution, civil, military, and religious, with the code of laws presented to them by the Deity, is contained in the books of Moses, and will afford us copious materials for future consideration. Their subsequent revolutions of government under Joshua, fifteen successive chiefs denominated judges, and a succession of kings, until they were first dismembered into two separate kingdoms, and after a lapse of some centuries both conquered by the Assyrians and Babylonians, and at the end of seventy years partially restored to their country and their temple, constitute the remaining historical books of the Old Testament, every part of which is full of instruction. But my present purpose is only to point your attention to their general historical character. My next will contain a few remarks on the Bible as a system of morals. In the meantime,

I remain your affectionate Father,

JOHN QUINCY ADAMS.

LETTER V.

In the promise with which my last letter to you upon the Bible was concluded, I undertook a task from the performance of which I have been hitherto deterred by its very magnitude and importance: the more I reflected upon the subject, the more sensibly did I feel my incompetency to do it justice, and by a weakness too common in the world, from the apprehension of inability to accomplish as much as I ought, I have hitherto been withheld from the attempt to accomplish anything at all. Thus more than a year has elapsed, leaving me still burdened with the load of my promise; and in now undertaking to discharge it, I must promise that you are only to expect the desultory and indigested thoughts which I have not the means of combining into a regular and systematic work.

I shall not entangle myself in the controversy which has sometimes been discussed with a temper not very congenial to either the nature of the question itself or the undoubted principles of Christianity, whether the Bible, like all other systems of morality, lays the ultimate basis of all human duties in *self-love*, or whether it enjoins duties on the principle of *perfect*, and *disinterested benevolence*. Whether the obligations are sanctioned by a promise of reward or a menace of punishment, the ultimate motive for its fulfilment may justly be attributed to selfish considerations. But if obedience to the will of God be the universal and only foundation of all moral duty, special injunctions may

be binding upon the consciences of men,
although their performance should not be
secured either by the impulse of hope or
fear. The law given from Sinai was a
civil and municipal as well as a moral
and religious code; it contained many
statutes adapted to that time only, and
to the particular circumstances of the nation to whom it was given; they could
of course be binding upon them, and only
upon them, until abrogated by the same
authority which enacted them, as they
afterward were by the Christian dispensation: but many others were of universal
application—laws essential to the existence of men in society, and most of which
have been enacted by every nation, which
ever professed any code of laws. But
the Levitical was given by God himself;
it extended to a great variety of objects
of infinite importance to the welfare of
men, but which could not come within

the reach of human legislation; it combined the temporal and spiritual authori-
ties together, and regulated not only the
actions but the passions of those to whom
it was given.   Human legislators can un-
dertake only to prescribe the actions of
men: they acknowledge their inability
to govern and direct the sentiments of the
heart; the very law styles it a rule of civil
conduct, not of internal principles, and
there is no crime in the power of an individual to perpetrate which he may not
design, project, and fully intend, without
incurring guilt in the eye of human law.
It is one of the greatest marks of Divine
favor bestowed upon the children of Israel,
that the legislator gave them rules not
only of action but for the government of
the heart.   There were occasionally a
few short sententious principles of morality issued from the oracles of Greece;
among them, and undoubtedly the most

excellent of them, was that of self-knowl-edge, which one of the purest moralists and finest poets of Rome expressly says came from Heaven.

But if you would remark the distin-guishing characteristics between true and false religion, compare the manner in which the ten commandments were proclaimed by the voice of the Almighty God, from Mount Sinai, with thunder, and lightning, and earthquake, by the sound of the trumpet, and in the hearing of six thousand souls, with the studied secresy, and mystery, and mummery, with which the Delphic and other oracles of the Gre-cian gods were delivered. The miracu-lous interpositions of Divine power re-corded in every part of the Bible, are in-variably marked with grandeur and sub-limity worthy of the Creator of the world, and before which the gods of Homer, not excepting his Jupiter, dwindle into the

most contemptible pigmies; but on no
occasion was the manifestation of the
Deity so solemn, so awful, so calculated
to make indelible impressions upon the
imaginations and souls of the mortals to
whom he revealed himself, as when he
appeared in the character of their Law-
giver. The law thus dispensed was,
however, imperfect; it was destined to
be partly suspended and improved into
absolute perfection many ages afterward
by the appearance of Jesus Christ upon
earth. But to judge of its excellence as
a system of laws, it must be compared
with human codes which existed or were
promulgated at nearly the same age of
the world in other nations. Remember,
that the law was given 1,490 years before
Christ was born, at the time the Assyrian
and Egyptian monarchies existed: but of
their government and laws we know
scarcely anything save what is collected

from the Bible. Of the Phrygian, Lydian, and Trojan states, at the same period, little more is known. The president Gorget, in a very elaborate and ingenious work on the origin of letters, arts, and sciences, among the ancient nations, says, that " the maxims, the civil and political laws of these people, are absolutely unknown; that not even an idea of them can be formed, with the single exception of the Lydians, of whom Herodotus asserts, that their laws were the same as the Greeks."—The same author contrasts the total darkness and oblivion into which all the institutions of these mighty empires have fallen, with the fulness and clearness and admirable composition of the Hebrew code, which has not only descended to us entire, but still continues the national code of the Jews (scattered as they are over the whole face of the earth), and enters so largely into the

legislation of almost every civilized nation upon the globe. He observes that
" these laws have been prescribed by God
himself: the merely human laws of other
contemporary nations can not bear any
comparison with them."

But my motive in forming the comparison, is to present to your reflections as a
proof—and to my mind a very strong
proof—of the reality of their divine origin:
for how is it that the whole system of
government, and administration, the municipal, political, ecclesiastical, military,
and moral laws and institutions, which
bound in society the numberless myriads
of human beings who formed for many
successive ages the stupendous monarchies of Africa and Asia, should have
perished entirely and been obliterated
from the memory of mankind, while the
laws of a paltry tribe of shepherds, char-
acterized by Tacitus, and the sneering

infidelity of Gibbon, as "the most despised portion of their slaves," should not only have survived the wreck of those empires, but remain to this day rules of faith and practice to every enlightened nation of the world, and perishable only with it? The reason is obvious: it is their intrinsic excellence which has preserved them from the destruction which befalls all the works of mortal man. The precepts of the decalogue alone (says Gorget), disclose more sublime truths, more maxims essentially suited to the happiness of man, than all the writings of profane antiquity put together can furnish. The more you meditate on the laws of Moses, the more striking and brighter does their wisdom appear. It would be a laborious but not an unprofitable investigation, to reduce into a regular classification, like that of the institutes of Justinian or the Commentaries of Blackstone, the

whole code of Moses, which embraces
not only all the ordinary subjects of legislation together with the principles of religion and morality, but laws of ecclesiastical directions concerning the minutest
actions and dress of individuals. This,
however, would lead me too far from my
present purpose, which is merely to consider the Bible as a system of morality ;
I shall therefore notice those parts of the
law which may be referred particularly
to that class, and at present must confine
myself to a few remarks upon the decalogue itself, which, having been spoken
by the voice, and twice written upon the
stone tables by the finger of God, may
be considered as the foundation of the
whole system—of the ten commandments,
emphatically so called, for the extraordinary and miraculous distinction by which
they were promulgated.

The first four commandments are religious laws, the fifth and tenth are properly and peculiarly moral and domestic rules; the other four are of the criminal department of municipal laws: the unity of the godhead, the prohibition of making graven images to worship: that of taking lightly (or in vain as the English translation expresses it) the name of the Deity, and the injunction to observe the Sabbath as a day sanctified and set apart for his worship, were all intended to inculcate the reverence for the one only and true God — that profound and penetrating sentiment of piety which, in a former letter, I urged as the great and only immovable foundation of all human virtue. Next to the duties toward the Creator, that of honoring the earthly parent is enjoined: it is to them that every individual owes the greatest obligations, and to them that he is consequently bound by the first and strongest of all earthly ties.

The following commands, applying to the
relations between man and his fellow
mortals, are all negative, as their application was universal, to every human being: it was not required that any positive
acts of beneficence toward them should
be performed; but only to abstain from
wronging them, either: first, in their persons: second, in their property; third, in
their conjugal rights; fourth, in their good
name: after which, all the essential enjoyments of life being thus guarded from
voluntary injury, the tenth and closing
commandment goes to the very source of
all human actions—the heart—and positively forbids all those desires which first
prompt and lead to every transgression
upon the property and right of our fellow-
creatures. Vain, indeed, would be the
search among the writings of profane antiquity (not merely of that remote antiquity, but even in the most refined and

philosophical ages of Greece and Rome),
to find so broad, so complete and so solid
a basis for morality as this decalogue lays
down. Yet I have said it was imperfect
—its sanctions, its rewards, its punishments, had reference only to present life,
and it had no injunctions of positive
beneficence toward our neighbors. Of
these the law was not entirely destitute
in its other parts; but, both in this respect and in the other, it was to be per-
fected by him who brought life and immortality to light in the gospel. Upon
which subject you shall hear more,

From your affectionate Father,

JOHN QUINCY ADAMS.

LETTER VI.

I PROMISED you, in my last letters, to state the particulars in which I deemed the Christian dispensation to be an improvement, or perfection of the law delivered at Sinai, considered as including a system of morality ; but before I come to this point, it is proper to remark upon the character of the books of the Old Testament, subsequent to those of Moses. Some are historical, some prophetical, and some poetical ; and two may be considered as peculiarly of the moral class —one being an affecting dissertation upon the vanity of human life, and another a collection of moral sentences under the

name of Proverbs. I have already observed that the great immovable and
eternal foundation of the superiority of
scripture morals, to all other morality,
was the idea of God disclosed in them
and only in them : the unity of God, his
omnipotence, his righteousness, his mercy, and the infinity of his attributes, are
marked in every line of the Old Testament, in characters which nothing less
than blindness, can fail to discern, and
nothing less than fraud can misrepre-
sent. This conception of God serving
as a basis for the piety of his worship-
pers, was of course incomparably more
rational and more profound, than it was
possible that sentiment could be which
adored devils for deities, or even that of
philosophers, like Socrates, Plato, and
Cicero, who with purer and more exalted
ideas of the Divine nature, than the rab-
ble of the poets, still considered the ex-

istence of any God at all, as a question upon which they could form no decided opinion. *You have seen that even Cicero believed the only solid foundation of all human virtue to be piety; and it was impossible that a piety so far transcending that of all other nations should not contain in its consequences a system of moral virtue equally transcendent.

The first of the ten commandments was, that the Jewish people should never admit the idea of any other God—the object of the second, third, and fourth, was merely to impress with greater force the obligation of the first, and to obviate the tendencies and temptations, which might arise to its being neglected, or disregarded. Throughout the whole law, the same injunctions are continually renewed; all the rites and ceremonies were adapted to root deeper into the hearts and souls of the chosen people, that the Lord Jehovah was to be for ever the sole and exclusive object of love. Reverence and adoration, unbounded as his own nature was the principle; every letter of the law, and the whole Bible is but a commentary upon it, and corollary from it. The law was given not merely in the form of a commandment from God, but in that of a covenant or compact between the Supreme Creator and the Jewish people; it was sanctioned by the blessing and the curse pronounced upon Mount Gerizim and Mount Ebal, in the presence of the whole Jewish people and strangers, and by the solemn acceptance of the whole people responding amen to every one of the curses denounced for violation on their part of the covenant. From that day until the birth of Christ (a period of about fifteen hundred years) the historical books of the Old Testament, are

no more than a simple record of the fulfilment of the covenant, in all its blessings and curses, exactly adapted to the
fulfilment or transgression of its duties
by the people. The nation was first
governed by Joshua, under the express
appointment of God; then by a succession of judges, and afterward by a double
line of kings, until conquered and carried into captivity by the kings of As-
syria and Babylon: seventy years afterward restored to their country, their temple, and their laws; and again conquered
by the Romans, and ruled by their tribu-
tary kings and proconsuls. Yet, through
all their vicissitudes of fortune, they never complied with the duties to which
they had bound themselves by the covenant, without being loaded with the
blessings promised on Mount Gerizim,
and never departed from them without
being afflicted with some of the curses

denounced upon Mount Ebal. The prophetical books are themselves historical
—for prophecy, in the strictest sense, is
no more than history related before the
event; but the Jewish prophets (of whom
there was a succession almost constant,
from the time of Joshua to that of Christ)
were messengers, specially commissioned
of God, to warn the people of their duty, to foretell the punishments which
awaited their transgressions, and finally
to keep alive by uninterrupted prediction
the expectation of the Messiah, "the
seed of Abraham, in whom all the families of the earth should be blessed."
With this conception of the Divine nature, so infinitely surpassing that of any
other nation—with this system of moral
virtue, so indissolubly blending as by the
eternal constitution of things must be
blended piety—with this uninterrupted
series of signs and wonders, prophets and

seers, miraculous interpositions of the omnipotent Creator, to preserve and vindicate the truth — it is lamentable ; but to those who know the nature of man, it is not surprising to find the Jewish history little else than a narrative of idolatries and corruption of the Israelites and their monarchs. That the very people who had heard the voice of God from Mount Sinai, within forty days compel Aaron to make a golden calf, and worship that as the " God who brought them out of the land of Egypt"—that the very Solomon, the wisest of mankind, to whom God had twice revealed himself in visions—the sublime dictator of the temple, the witness, in the presence of the whole people, of the fire from heaven which consumed the offerings from the altar, and of the glory of the Lord that filled the house—that he, in his old age, beguiled by fair idolatresses, should have fallen from the worship of the ever-blessed Jehovah, to that of Ashtaroth and Milcom, &c., the abomination of all the petty tribes of Judea—that of Baal, and Dagon, &c., the sun, moon, and planets, and all the host of heaven—that the mountains and plains, every high place and every grove, should have swarmed with idols, to corrupt the hearts and debase the minds of a people so highly favored of Heaven, the elect of the Almighty—may be among the mysteries of Divine Providence, which it is not given to mortality to explain, but is inadmissible only to those who presume to demand why it has pleased the Supreme Arbiter of events, to create such a being as man. Observe, however, that amid the atrocious crimes which that nation so often polluted themselves with—through all their servitudes, dismemberments, captivities, and transmigrations—the Di-

vine light, which had been imparted exclusively to them, was never extinguish-
ed; the law delivered from Sinai, was
preserved in all purity; the histories
which attested its violations and its ac-
complishments were recorded and never
lost. The writings of the prophets, of
David, and Solomon, were all inspired
with the same idea of the Godhead, the
same intertwinement of religion and morality, and the same anticipations of the
divine "Immanuel, the God with us;"
these survived all the changes of government and of constitutions which befell the
people: "the pillar of cloud by day, and
the pillár of fire by night,"—the law and
the prophets, eternal in their nature—
went before them unsullied, and unim-
paired through all the ruins of rebellion
and revolution, of conquest and disper-
sion, of war, pestilence, and famine.
The Assyrian, Babylonian, and Egyptian

empires, Tyre and Sidon, Carthage, and all the other nations of antiquity, rose and fell in their religious institutions at the same time as in their laws and government: it was the practice of the Romans, when they besieged a city, to invoke its gods to come over to them; they considered the gods as summer friends, ready to desert their votaries in the hour of calamity, or as traitors, ready to sell themselves for a bribe; they had no higher estimate of their own than of the stranger deities, whom, as Gibbon said—"they were always ready to admit to the freedom of the city." All the gods of the heathens have perished with their makers; for where on the face of the globe, could now be found the being who believes in any one of them? So much more deep and strong was the hold which the God of Abraham, Isaac, and Jacob, took upon the imaginations and

reason of mankind, that I might almost in-
vert the question, and say, "Where is the
human being found believing in any God
at all, and not believing in him?"

The moral character of the Old Testament, then, is, that piety to God is the
foundation of all virtue, and that virtue
is inseparable from it: but that piety
without the practice of virtue is itself a
crime and the aggravation of all iniquity.
All the virtues which are here recognised
by the heathen, are inculcated not only
with more authority but with more energy of argument and more eloquent persuasion in the Bible than in all the writings of the ancient moralists.   In one of
the apocryphal books (Wisdom of Solomon), the cardinal virtues are expressly
named: "If any man love righteousness,
her labors are virtue, for she teacheth
temperance, and prudence, and justice,
and fortitude;" which are such things as

men ean have nothing more profitable in
this life. The book of Job, whether
considered as history or as an allegorical
parable, was written to teach the lessons
of patience under afflictions, of resignation
under Divine chastisement, of undoubted
confidence in the justice and goodness of
God under every temptation or provoca-
tion to depart from it. The morality of
the apocryphal books is generally the
same as that of the inspired writers, except that in some of them there is more
stress laid upon the minor objects of the
law, and merely formal ordinances of
police, and less continual recurrence to
"the weightier matters."—The book of
Ecclesiasticus, however, contains ,more
wisdom than all the sayings of the seven
Grecian sages. It was upon this foundation that the more perfect system of
Christian morality was to be raised.—
But I must defer the consideration to my

next letter. In the meantime as I have urged that the scriptural idea of God is the foundation of all perfect virtue, and that it is totally different from the idea of God conceived by any ancient nation, I should recommend it to you in pursuing the Scriptures hereafter to meditate often upon the expressions by which they mark the character of the Deity, and to reflect upon the duties to him and to your fellow mortals which follow by inevitable deductions from them. That you may have an exact idea of the opinions of ancient heathen philosophers concerning God, or *rather the gods*, study Cicero's dialogues, and read the abbe Olivet's remarks on the theology of the Grecian philosophers, annexed to his translations.

From your affectionate Father,

JOHN QUINCY ADAMS.

LETTER VII.

THE imperfections of the Mosaic institution which it was the object of Christ's mission upon earth to remove, appear to me to have been these: first, The want of a sufficient sanction. The rewards and penalties of the Levitical law had all a reference to the present life. There are many passages in the Old Testament which imply a state of existence after death, and some which directly assert a future state of retribution; but none of these were contained in the delivery of the law. At the time of Christ's advent, it was so far from being a settled article of the Jewish faith, that it was a subject of bitter controversy between the two principal sects—of Pharisees who believed in, and Sadducees who denied it. It was the special purpose of Christ's appearance upon earth, to bring immortality to light. He substituted the rewards and punishments of a future state of existence in the room of all others. The Jewish sanctions were exclusively temporal: those of Christ exclusively spiritual. Second, The want of universality. The Jewish dispensation was exclusively confined to a small and obscure nation. The purposes of the Supreme Creator in restricting the knowledge of himself to one petty herd of Egyptian slaves, are as inaccessible to our intelligence as those of his having concealed from them, and from the rest of mankind, the certain knowledge of their own immortality; yet the fact is unquestionable. The mission of Christ was intended to

communicate to the whole human race
all the permanent advantages of the Mosaic law, superadding to them—upon the
condition of repentance—the kingdom
of heaven, the blessing of eternal life.
Third, the complexity of the objects of
legislation. I have observed in a former
letter, that the law from Sinai comprised,
not only all the ordinary subjects of reg-
ulation for human societies, but those
which human legislators can not reach.
It was a civil law, a municipal law,
an ecclesiastical law, a law of police,
and a law of morality and religion:
it prohibited murder, adultery, theft,
and perjury; it prescribed rules for the
thoughts as well as for the actions of
men. The complexity, however prac-
ticable and even suitable for one small
national society, could not have attained
to all the families of the earth. The
parts of the Jewish law adapted to pro-

mote the happiness of mankind, under
every variety of situation and government in which they can be placed, were
all recognised and adopted by Christ;
and he expressly separated them from
the rest. He disclaimed all interference
with the ordinary objects of human legislation; he declared that his " kingdom
was not of this world;" he acknowledged
the authority of the Jewish magistrates;
he paid for his own person the tribute to
the Romans; he refused in more than one
instance to assume the office of judge in
matters of legal controversy; he strictly
limited the object of his own precepts
and authority to religion and morals; he
denounced no temporal punishment; he
promised no temporal rewards; he took
up man as a governable being, where the
human magistrate is compelled to leave
him, and supplied both precept of virtue
and motive for practising it, such as no

other moralist or legislator ever attempt-
ed to introduce.   Fourth, the burdensome
duties of positive rites, minute formalities,
and expensive sacrifices.   All these had
a tendency, not only to establish and
maintain the separation of the Jews from
all other nations, but in process of time
had been mistaken by the scribes, and
Pharisees, and lawyers, and probably by
the body of the people, for the substance
of religion.   All the rites were abolished
by Christ, or (as Paul expresses it)
"were nailed to his cross."   You will
recollect that I am now speaking of
Christianity, not as the scheme of redemption to mankind from the consequences of original sin, but as a system of
morality for regulating the conduct of
men while on earth; and the most striking and extraordinary feature of its character in this respect, is its tendency and
exhortations to absolute perfection.   The

language of Christ to his disciples is explicit: "Be ye therefore perfect, even as your father in heaven is perfect"— and this he enjoins at the conclusion of that precept, so expressly laid down, and so unanswerably argued, to "love their enemies, to bless those who cursed them, and pray for those who despitefully used and persecuted them." He seems to consider the temper of benevolence in return for injury, as constituting of itself a perfection similar to that of the Divine nature. It is undoubtedly the greatest conquest which the spirit of man can achieve over its infirmities; and to him who can attain that elevation of virtue which it requires, all other victories over the evil passions must be comparatively easy. Nor was the absolute perfection merely preached by Christ as a doctrine: it was practised by himself throughout his life; practised to the last instant of his agony on the cross; practised under circumstances of trial, such as no other human being was ever exposed to. He proved by his own example the possibility of that virtue which he taught; and although possessed of miraculous powers sufficient to control all the laws of nature, he expressly and repeatedly declined the use of them to save himself from any part of the sufferings which he was able to endure.

The sum of Christian morality, then, consists in piety to God, and benevolence to man: piety, manifested, not by formal, solemn rites and sacrifices of burnt-offerings, but by repentance, by obedience, by submission, by humility, by the worship of the heart, and by benevolence; not founded upon selfish motives, but superior even to a sense of wrong, or the resentment of injuries. Worldly prudence is scarcely noticed among all the instructions of Christ: the pursuit of honors and riches, the objects of ambition and avarice, are strongly discountenanced in many places: and an undue solicitude about the ordinary cares of life is occasionally reproved. Of worldly prudence, there are rules enough in the Proverbs of Solomon, and in the compilations of the son of Sirach; Christ passes no censure upon them, but he left what I call the selfish virtues where he found them. It was not to proclaim common-place morality that he came down from Heaven; his commands were new; that his disciples should "love one another," that they should love even strangers, that they should "love their enemies." He prescribed barriers against all the maleficient passions; he gave as a law, the utmost point of perfection of which human powers are susceptible, and at the same time allowed degrees of indulgence and relaxation to human frailty, proportioned to the power of any individual. An eminent writer in support of Christianity (Dr. Paley) expresses the opinion, that the direct object of the Christian revelation was to supply *motives*, and not *rules—sanctions*, and not *precepts;* and he strongly intimates that, independent of the purpose of Christ's atonement and propitiation for the sins of the world, the only object of his mission upon earth was to reveal a future state, "to bring life and immortality to light." He does not appear to think that Christ promulgated any new principle of morality; and he positively asserts that "morality, neither in the gospel nor in any other book, can be a subject of discovery, because qualities of actions depend entirely on their effects, which effects, must all along have been the subjects of human experience." To this I reply in the express words of

Jesus: "A *new* commandment I give you, that ye love one another;" and I add, that this command explained, illustrated, and dilated, as it was by the whole tenor of his discourses, and especially by the parable of the good Samaritan, appears to me to be not only entirely new, but, in the most rigorous sense of the word, a discovery in morals; and a discovery, the importance of which to the happiness of the human race, as far exceeds any discovery in the physical laws of nature, as the soul is superior to the body. If it be objected that the principles of benevolence toward enemies, and the forgiveness of injuries, may be found not only in the Old Testament, but even in some of the heathen writers, particularly the discourses of Socrates. I answer, that the same may be said of the immortality of the soul, and of the rewards and punishments of a future state. The doctrine was not more a discovery than the precept; but their connexion with each other, the authority with which they were taught, and the miracles by which they were enforced, belong exclusively to the mission of Christ. Attend particularly to the miracle recorded in the second chapter of Luke, as having taken place as the birth of Jesus; when the angel of the Lord said to the shepherds: "Fear nor, for behold 1 bring you glad tidings of great joy, which shall be to all people; for unto you is born this day in the city of David, a Savior, who is Christ the Lord." In these words the character of Jesus, as a Redeemer, was announced; but the historian adds—"And suddenly there was with the angel a multitude of the heavenly host praising God and singing, glory to God in the highest, and on earth peace, good will toward men." These words, as I understand them, an-

nounced the moral precept of benevolence
as explicitly for the object of Christ's appearance, as the preceding words had
declared the purpose of redemption. It
is related in the life of the Roman dra-
matic poet, Terence, that when one of
the personages of his comedy, the " Self-
Tormentor," the first time uttered on
the stage the line " Homo sum, humani
nil alienum puto" (1 am a man, nothing
human is uninteresting to me), a universal
shout of applause burst forth from the
whole audience, and that in so great a
multitude of Romans, and deputies from
the nations, their subjects and allies, there
was not one individual but felt in his
heart this noble sentiment. Yet how
feeble and defective it is, in comparison
with the Christian command of charity
as unfolded in the discoveries of Christ
and enlarged upon in the writings of his
apostles. The heart of man will always

respond with rapture to this sentiment when there is no selfish or unsocial passion to oppose it: but the command to lay it down as the great and fundamental rule of conduct for human life, and to subdue and sacrifice all the tyrannical and selfish passions to preserve it, this is the peculiar and unfading glory of Christianity; this is the conquest over ourselves, which, without the aid of a merciful God, none of us can achieve, and which it was worthy of his special interposition to enable us to accomplish.

From your affectionate Father,
JOHN QUINCY ADAMS.

LETTER VIII.

THE whole system of Christianity appears to have been set forth by its Divine Author in his sermon on the mount, recorded in the fifth, sixth, and seventh chapters of Matthew. I intend hereafter to make them the subject of remarks, much more at large; for the present, I confine myself merely to general views. What I would impress upon your mind, is infinitely important to the happiness and virtue of your life, as the general spirit of Christianity, and the duties which results from it. In my last letter, I showed you, from the very words of our Savior, that he commanded his disciples to aim at absolute perfection, and that this perfection consisted in self-subjugation and brotherly love, in the complete conquest of our own passions, and in the practice of benevolence to our fellow-creatures. Among the Grecian systems of moral philosophy, that of the Stoics resembles the Christian doctrine in the particular of requiring the total subjugation of the passions; and this part of the Stoic principles was adopted by the academies. You will find the question discussed with all the eloquence and ingenuity of Cicero, in the fourth of his Tusculan disputations, which I advise you to read and meditate upon. You will there find proved, the duty of subduing the passions. It is sometimes objected that this theory is not adapted to the infirmities of human nature; that it is not made for a being so constituted as man; that an earthen vessel is not formed to dash itself against a rock; that in yielding to the impulses of the passions, man only follows the dictates of his nature; that to subdue them entirely, is an effort beyond his powers. The weakness and frailty of our nature, it is not possible to deny—it is too strongly tested by all human experience, as well as by the whole tenor of the Scriptures; but the degree of weakness must be measured by the efforts to overcome it, and not by indulgence to it. Once admit weakness as an argument to forbear exertion, and it results in absolute impotence. It is also very inconclusive reasoning to infer, that because perfection is not absolutely to be obtained, it is therefore not to be sought. Human excellence consists in approximation to perfection: and the only means of approaching to any term, is by endeavoring to obtain the term itself. With these convictions upon the mind—with a sincere and honest effort to practise upon them, and with the aid of a divine blessing, which is promised to it, the approaches to perfection may at least be so great, as to nearly answer all the ends which absolute perfection itself could attain. All exertion, therefore, is virtue; and if the tree be judged by its fruit, it is certain that all the most virtuous characters of heathen antiquity, were the disciples of the Stoic doctrine. But let it even be admitted that a perfect command of the passions is unattainable to human infirmity, it will still be true, that the degree of moral excellence possessed by any individual, is in exact proportion to the degree of control he exercises over himself. According to the Stoics, all vice was resolvable into folly: according to the Christian principle it is all the effect of weakness. In order to preserve the dominion of our own passions, it behooves us to be constantly and strictly on our guard against the influence and infection of the passions of others. This caution above all is necessary to youth; and I deem it indispensable to enjoin it upon you — because, as kindness and benevolence comprise the whole system of Christian duties, there may be, and often is, great danger of falling into errors and vice, merely for the want of energy to resist the example or enticement of others. On this point the true character of Christian morality appears to me to have been misunderstood by some of its ablest and warmest defenders.

In Paley's "View of the Evidences of Christianity," there is a chapter upon the morality of the gospel, the general tenor, of which (as of the whole work) is excellent, but in which there is the following passage: "There are two opposite descriptions of character, under

which mankind may generally be class-
ed: the one possesses vigor, firmness,
resolution, is active and daring, quick in
its sensibilities, jealous of its fame, eager
in its attachments, inflexible of its purposes, violent in its resentment; the other
meek, yielding, complying, forgiving, not
prompt to act, but willing to suffer, silent
and gentle under rudeness and insults,
suing for reconciliation, where others
would demand satisfaction; giving away
to the pushes of impudence, conceding and
indulgent to the prejudices, the wrong-
headedness, the intractability of others,
with whom it has to deal. The former
of these characters is, and ever has been,
the favorite of the world; it is the character of great men—there is a dignity in
it which commands respect. The latter
is poor-spirited, tame, and abject. Yet,
so it has happened, that with the founder
of Christianity, the latter is the subject of

his commendation, his precepts, his example, and that the former is so in no part of its composition. Dr. Paley in this place adopts the opinion of Soame Jennings, whose essay on the "Internal Evidences of Christianity" he strongly recommends; but I can not consider it either as an accurate and discerning delineation of character, nor as exhibiting a correct representation of Christian principles. The founder of Christianity did indeed pronounce distinct and positive blessings upon the "poor in spirit," which is by no means synonymous with the "poor-spirited;" and upon the meek; but in what part of the gospel did Dr. Paley find him countenancing by "commendation, by precept or example, the tame and abject"? The character which Christ assumed upon earth, was that of a Lord and Master; it was in that character his disciples received and acknowledged him. The obedience he required was unbounded, infinitely beyond that which was ever claimed by the most absolute earthly sovereign of his subjects: never for one moment did he recede from this authoritative station; he preserved it in washing the feet of his disciples; he preserved it in answer to the officer who struck him for this very deportment to the high-priest; he preserved it in the agony of his ejaculation on the cross, "Father, forgive them, for they know not what they do." He expressly declared himself, "the Prince of this world, and the Son of God." He spoke as one having authority, not only to his disciples, but to his mother, to his judges, to Pilate the Roman governor, to John the Baptist, his precursor; and there is not in the four gospels, one act, not one word recorded of him (excepting his communion with God), that was not a direct or im-

plied assertion of authority. He said to
his disciples, " Learn of me, for I am
meek and lowly of heart," &c.; but
where did he ever say to them, " Learn of
me, for I am tame and abject" ? There is
certainly nothing more strongly marked
in the precepts and examples of Christ,
than the principle of stubborn and inflexible resistance against the impulses of
others to evil. He taught his disciples
to renounce everything that is counted
enjoyment upon earth ; " to take up their
cross," and to suffer ill-treatment, perse-
cution, and death, for his sake. What
else is the book of the " Acts of the
Apostles," than a record of the faith-
fulness with which these chosen ministers
of the gospel carried these injunctions
into execution ? In the conduct and
speeches of Peter, John, and Paul, is
there anything that could justly be
called " tame or abject" ? Is there any-

thing indicating a resemblance to the second class of character into which Dr. Paley divides all mankind? If there is a character upon historical record distinguished by a bold, inflexible, tenacious, and intrepid spirit, it is that of Paul. It was to such characters only, that the commission to " teach all nations," could be committed with certainty of success. Observe the impression of Christ, in his charge to Peter (a rock): " And upon this rock I will build my church, and the gates of hell shall not prevail against it." Dr. Paley's Christian is one of those drivellers, who, to use a vulgar phrase, can never say no, to anybody. The true Christian is the " Justum et tenacem propositi virum" of Horace, (" the man who is just and steady to his purpose"). The combination of these qualities so essential to heroic character, with those of meekness, lowliness of heart, and broth-

erly love, is what constitutes that moral
perfection of which Christ gave an example in his own life, and to which he
commands his disciples to aspire. Endeavor, my dear son, to discipline your
heart, and to govern your conduct by
these principles thus combined; be meek,
be gentle, be kindly affectionate to all
mankind, not excepting your enemies;
but never be "tame or abject;" never
give way to the pushes of impudence, or
show yourself yielding or complying to
prejudice, wrong-headedness, or intractability, which would lead or draw you
astray from the dictates of your own conscience, and your own sense of right:
"till you die, let not your integrity depart from you:" build your house upon
the rock, and then let the rains descend,
and the floods come, and the winds
blow and beat upon that house—"it shall
not fall, it will be founded upon a rock."

So promises your blessed Lord and Master, and so prays your affectionate Father.

JOHN QUINCY ADAMS.

LETTER IX.

THE fourth and last point of view in which I proposed to offer you some general observations upon the Scriptures, was with reference to literature; and the first remark that presents itself is, that the five books of Moses, are the most ancient monuments of written language now extant in the world; the book of Job is nearly of the same date, and by many of the Jewish and Christian commentators, is thought to have been written by Moses. The employment of alphabetical characters to represent all the articulations of the human voice, is the greatest invention that ever was compassed by human

genius. Plato says that "it was the discovery of either a God, or a man divinely
inspired." The Egyytians ascribed it to
Thot, whom the Greeks afterward worshipped under the name of Hermes.
This is, however, a fabulous origin.
That it was an Egyptian invention, there
is little doubt; and it was a part of that
learning of the Egyptians, in all of which
we are told, "Moses was versed."
It is probable that when Moses wrote,
this act was, if not absolutely recent, of
no very remote invention. There was
but one copy of the law written in a
book. It was deposited in the ark of the
covenant, and was read aloud once in
seven years, to all the people, at their
general assembly in the feast of taber-
nacles. There was one other copy of
the law, written upon stone, erected on
Mount Ebal. It does not appear that
there existed any other copies. In pro-

cess of time the usage of reading it thus must have been dropped, and the monument upon Mount Ebal must have perished; for in the reign of Josiah, about eight hundred years afterward, the book of the law was found in the temple. How long it had been lost is not expressly told; but from the astonishment and consternation of Josiah upon hearing the book read, its contents must have been long forgotten so that scarcely a tradition of them remained. We are indeed told, that, when the ark of the covenant was deposited in the temple of Solomon, there was nothing in the ark save the two tables, which Moses put therein at Horeb. The two tables contained not the whole law, but the ten commandments: the book of the law was therefore no longer in the ark, at the dedication of Solomon's temple; that is, about five hundred years after the law was given, and three hun-

dred before the book was found by Hez-
ekiah the high-priest, in the eighteenth
year of Josiah. From these circumstances, as well as from the expedients
used by Moses and Joshua for preserving
the ceremonial law, and the repeated
covenant between God and the people, it
is observed that the art and practice of
writing was extremely rare, and that
very few of the people were even taught
to read; that there were few books extant, and of those few, only single copies;
the art of writing, speaking, and thinking, with their several modifications of
grammar, rhetoric, and logic, were never
cultivated among the Hebrews, as they
were (though not till a thousand years
later than Moses) among the Greeks.
Philosophical research and the spirit of
analysis appear to have belonged among
the ancient nations, exclusively to the
Greeks; they studied language as a sci-

ence, and from the discoveries they made in this pursuit, resulted a system of literary compositions, founded upon logical deductions. The language of the ancient writers was not constructed upon the foundation of abtruse science; it partakes of the nature of all primitive languages, which is almost entirely figurative; and in some degree of the character of primitive writing and hieroglyphics. We are not told from what materials Moses compiled the book of Genesis (which contains the history of the creation, and of three hundred years succeeding it, and which terminates three generations prior to the birth of Moses himself), whether he had it altogether from tradition, or whether he collected it from the more ancient written or printed memorials. The account of the creation, of the fall of man, and all the antediluvian part of the history, carries strong internal evidences of having been copied or (if I may express myself) translated from hieroglyphic or symbolical record; the story is of the most perfect simplicity, the discourses of the persons introduced, are given as if taken down verbatim, from their mouths, and the narrative is scarcely anything more than the connecting link of the discourses; the genealogies are given with great precision; and, this is one of the most remarkable peculiarities of the Old Testament; the rest is all figurative; the rib, the garden, the tree of life, and of the knowledge of good and evil, the apple, the serpent, are all images which seem to indicate a hieroglyphic origin. All the historical books, of both the Old and New Testaments, retain the peculiar characteristics that I have noticed; the simplicity and brevity of the narrative, the practice of repeating all discourses in the identical words spoken,

and the constant use of figurative symbolical and allegorical language. But of
the rules of composition, prescribed by
the Grecian schools, the unities of Aris-
totle, or the congruities of figures taught
by the Greek philologists, not a feature is
to be seen. The Psalms are a collection
of songs ; the Song of Solomon is a pas-
toral poem ; the Proverbs are a collection
of moral sentences and maxims, appa-
rently addressed by Solomon *to* his son,
with the addition of others of the same
description; the prophetical books are
partly historical and partly poetical—
they contain the narrative of visions and
revelations of the Deity to the prophets,
who recorded them.

In the New Testament, the four gospels and the Acts of the Apostles are
historical—they contain memoirs of the
life of Christ, and some of his disciples,
and the proceedings of some of his prin-

cipal apostles, for some years after his decease. The simplicity of the narrative, is the same as that of the Old Testament; the style in general, indicates an age when reading and writing, had become more common, and books more multiplied. The Epistles of Paul, are the productions of a mind educated in the learning of the age, and well versed in the Grecian literature; from his history, it appears that he was not only capable of maintaining an argument with the doctors of the Jewish law, but of discussing principles with the Stoic and Epicurean philosophers; his speech at Athens is a specimen of eloquence worthy of an audience in the native country of Demosthenes. The Apocalypse of John resembles, in many respects, some of the prophetical books of the Old Testament; the figurative, symbolical, and allegorical language of these books shows a range of imagination suitable only to be the record of dreams and visions—their language is in many parts inexplicably obscure. It has been, and it is to this day, among the follies and vices of many sects of Christians, to attempt explanations of them, adapted to sectarian purposes and opinions. The style of none of the books, of either the Old or New Testament, affords a general model for imitation to a writer of the present age ; the principles and rules for composition derived from Greek and Roman schools, and the example of their principal writers, have been so generally adopted in modern literature, that the Scriptures—differing so essentially from them—could not be imitated without great affectation ; but for pathos of narrative ; for the selections of incidents that go directly to the heart ; for the picturesque of character and manner ; the selection of circumstances that mark the individuality of persons; for copiousness, grandeur, and sublimity of imagery; for unanswerable cogency and closeness of reasoning; and for irresistible force of persuasion: no book in the world deserves to be so unceasingly studied, and so profoundly meditated upon as the Bible.

I shall conclude here the series of letters which I proposed, about two years ago, to write you for the purpose of exhorting you to search the Scriptures, and of pointing out to your consideration the general points of application; with a view to which, I thought this study might be made profitable to the improvement and usefulness of your future life. There are other and particular points to which I may hereafter occasionally invite your attention. I am sensible how feeble and superficial what I have written has been, and every letter has con-

vinced me more and more of my own incompetency to the adequate performance
of the task I had assumed; but my
great object was to show you the importance of devoting your own faculties to
this pursuit; to read the Bible is of itself
a laudable occupation and can scarcely
fail of being a useful employment of time;
but the habit of reflecting upon what you
have read is equally essential as that of
reading itself, to give it all the efficacy
of which it is susceptible. I therefore
recommend to you to set apart a small
portion of every day to read one or more
chapters of the Bible, and always read it
with reference to some particular train
of observation or reflection. In these
letters, I have suggested to you four
general ones. Considering the Scriptures as Divine Revelations; as historical records; as a system of morals; and
as literary compositions. There are

many other points of view in which they may be subjects of useful investigation. As an expedient for fixing your attention, make it also a practice for some time, to minute down in writing your reflections upon what you read from day to day; you may perhaps at first find this irksome, and your reflections scanty and unimportant, but they will soon become both easy and copious. Be careful of all not to let your reading make you a pedant, or a bigot; let it never puff you up with pride or a conceited opinion of your own knowledge, nor make you intolerant of the opinions which others draw from the same source, however different from your own. And may the merciful Creator, who gave the Scriptures for our instruction, bless your study of them, and make them to you "fruitful of good works." Your affectionate Father,

JOHN QUINCY ADAMS.

[IN 1840, Mr. MORGAN, the present secretary of state of New York, occupied a seat in Congress next to that of Mr. ADAMS. Several young ladies in Mr. OGLE's district had requested Mr. ADAMS's autograph. In complying with that request, Mr. ADAMS added the following poem, a copy of which Mr. MORGAN obtained. Mr. ADAMS, be it remembered, when this spirited poem was written, had attained his 74th year.]

THE WANTS OF MAN.

BY JOHN QUINCY ADAMS.

> " Man wants but little here below,
> Nor wants that little long."
> *Goldsmith's Hermit.*

I.

"Man wants but little here below,
  Nor wants that little long."
'T is not with *me* exactly so —
  But 't is so in the song.
My wants are many, and, if told,
  Would muster many a score ;
And were each wish a mint of gold,
  I still should long for more.

II.

What first I want is daily bread,
  And canvas-backs and wine,
And all the realms of nature spread
  Before me when I dine :
Four courses scarcely can provide
  My appetite to quell,
With four choice cooks from France beside,
  To dress my dinner well.

III.

What next I want, at heavy cost,
  Is elegant attire —
Black sable furs for winter's frost,
  And silks for summer's fire,
And Cashmere shawls and Brussels lace
  My bosom's front to deck,
And diamond rings my hands to grace,
  And rubies for my neck.

IV.

And then I want a mansion fair,
  A dwelling-house in style,
Four stories high, for wholesome air,
  A massive marble pile :
With halls for banquets and for balls
  All furnished rich and fine ;
With stabled studs in fifty stalls,
  And cellars for my wine.

V.

I want a garden and a park
  My dwelling to surround —
A thousand acres (bless the mark !)
  With walls encompassed round,
Where flocks may range and herds may low,
  And kids and lambkins play —
And flowers and fruits commingled grow,
  All Eden to display.

VI.

I want, when summer's foliage falls,
  And autumn strips the trees,
A house within the city's walls,
  For comfort and for ease —
But here, as space is somewhat scant,
  And acres rather rare,
My house in town I only want
  To occupy —— a square.

VII.

I want a steward, butler, cooks,
    A coachman, footman, grooms,
A library of well-bound books,
    And picture-garnished rooms —
Correggios, Magdalen, and Night,
    The Matron of the chair —
Guido's fleet-courses in their flight,
    And Claudes, at least a pair.

VIII.

I want a cabinet profuse
    Of medals, coins, and gems ;
A printing-press, for private use,
    Of fifty thousand *ems*,
And plants, and minerals, and shells —
    Worms, insects, fishes, birds,
And every beast on earth that dwells
    In solitude or herds.

IX

I want a board of burnished plate,
    Of silver and of gold —
Tureens of twenty pounds in weight,
    With sculpture's richest mould —
Plateaus with chandeliers and lamps,
    Plates, dishes, all the same,
And porcelain vases with the stamps
    Of Sevres, Angouleme.

X.

And maples of fair glossy stain
    Must form my chamber-doors,
And carpets of the Wilton grain
    Must cover all my floors ;
My walls with tapestry bedecked
    Must never be outdone,
And damask curtains must protect
    Their colors from the sun.

XI.

And mirrors of the largest pane
  From Venice must be brought,
And sandal-wood and bamboo-cane
  For chairs and tables bought;
On all the mantelpieces, clocks
  Of thrice-gilt bronze must stand,
And screens of ebony and box
  Invite the stranger's hand.

XII.

I want — (who does not want?) — a wife,
  Affectionate and fair,
To solace all the woes of life,
  And all its joys to share —
Of temper sweet, of yielding will,
  Of firm yet placid mind —
With all my faults to love me still,
  With sentiment refined.

XIII.

And as Time's car incessant runs,
  And Fortune fills my store,
I want of daughters and of sons
  From eight to half a score:
I want (alas! can mortal dare
  Such bliss on earth to crave?)
That all the girls be chaste and fair —
  The boys all wise and brave.

XIV.

And when my bosom's darling sings
  With melody divine,
A pedal-harp of many strings
  Must with her voice combine:
A piano, exquisitively wrought,
  Must open stand, apart,
That all my daughters may be taught
  To win the stranger's heart.

XV.

My wife and daughters will desire
  Refreshment from perfumes,
Cosmetic for the skin require,
  And artificial blooms :
The civet, fragrance shall dispense
  And treasured sweets return —
Cologne revive the flagging sense,
  And smoking amber burn.

XVI.

And when, at night, my weary head
  Begins to droop and doze,
A southern chamber holds my bed
  For nature's soft repose :
With blankets, counterpanes, and sheet,
  Mattress and bed of down,
And comfortables for my feet,
  And pillows for my crown.

XVII.

I want a warm and faithful friend
  To cheer the adverse hour,
Who ne'er to flatter will descend
  Nor bend the knee to power —
A friend to chide me when I'm wrong,
  My inmost soul to see,
And that my friendship proves as strong
  For him as his for me.

XVIII.

I want a kind and tender heart
  For others' wants to feel,
A soul secure from Fortune's dart,
  And bosom armed with steel —
To bear divine chastisement's rod,
  And mingling, in my plan,
Submission to the will of God
  With charity to man.

XIX.

I want a keen, observing eye —
  An ever-listening ear,
The truth through all disguise to spy,
  And wisdom's voice to hear :
A tongue to speak at virtue's need,
  In Heaven's sublimest strain,
And lips the cause of man to plead,
  And never plead in vain.

XX.

I want uninterrupted health
  Throughout my long career ;
And streams of never-failing wealth
  To scatter far and near,
The destitute to clothe and feed,
  Free bounty to bestow —
Supply the helpless orphan's need
  And sooth the widow's wo.

XXI.

I want the genius to conceive,
  The talents to unfold
Designs, the vicious to retrieve —
  The virtuous to uphold :
Inventive power, combining skill,
  A persevering soul,
Of human hearts to mould the will
  And reach from pole to pole.

XXII.

I want the seals of power and place,
  The ensigns of command —
Charged by the people's unbought grace,
  To rule my native land :
Nor crown, nor sceptre, would I ask,
  But from my country's will,
By day, by night, to ply the task
  Her cup of bliss to fill.

XXIII.

I want the voice of honest praise
  To follow me behind,
And to be thought in future days
  The friend of human kind —
That after-ages, as they rise,
  Exulting may proclaim,
In choral union to the skies,
  Their blessings on my name.

XXIV.

These are the wants of mortal man:
  I can not want them long,
For life itself is but a span
  And earthly bliss a song.
My last great want, absorbing all,
  Is, when beneath the sod,
And summoned to my final call,
  The *mercy of my God.*

XXV.

And oh! while circles in my veins
  Of life the purple stream,
And yet a fragment small remains
  Of nature's transient dream,
My soul, in humble hope unscarred,
  Forget not thou to pray,
That this thy *want* may be prepared
  To meet the Judgment-day!

THE END.

CPSIA information can be obtained
at www.ICGtesting.com
Printed in the USA
BVHW041317270221
601217BV00003B/201